# THE HAUNTING OF THE ANOKA MASONIC LODGE

## BY JUNE GOSSLER ANDERSON

June Gossler Anderson

Copyright 2015 June Gossler Anderson

Andover, Minnesota

ISBN: 9780984488544

All rights reserved. No part of this book may be reproduced or transmitted in any form or by any means, electronic or mechanical, including photocopying, recording, or by any information storage and retrieval system without written permission from the author, except for the inclusion of brief quotations in a review.

Cover design: Todd Anderson
Layout, formatting, and printing: Todd Anderson

Published by Grannygirlpress
www.grannygirlpress.com

The Haunting of the Anoka Masonic Lodge

# Dedicated

# To the Spirit and Spirits of Freemasonry

## Acknowledgements:

I would like to thank:

- My anonymous friend (you know who you are) who was the catalyst for this book;

- The Freemasons, members of the Order of Eastern Star, and Job's Daughters whose stories are the heart of this book;

- The staff of the Anoka County Historical Society (ACHS) whose documentation of encounters with the unexplained are a part of the Anoka Ghost Tour lore as well as that of their old home, Colonial Hall;

- Mary Mestelle and Deb Mucklow, past owners of the Artique, and the new owners of its successor, The Big White House, for sharing their stories;

- Josh Fulwider and Kevin Swanson, intrepid paranormal investigators who, through their expertise and with the help of technology, give us a glimpse into another world;

- Tom Malone for taking book-worthy photos of the Masonic Lodge, its interior, the investigative personnel, and their equipment.

- Gail Kishish for her eagle-eyed proofreading

- And most of all, John Freeburg, historian for the Anoka Masonic Lodge for making this book possible.

The Haunting of the Anoka Masonic Lodge

## **Forward**

As a volunteer for the Anoka County Historical Society (ACHS) I have been leading ghost tours through the darkened streets of Anoka since the fall of 2007 and since 2009, writing stories of its past life in the history column of the *Anoka Union,* now the *Anoka County Union Herald.* A question frequently asked me regarding the ghost tours is, "Have *you* ever seen a ghost?" I must admit that up until January of 2015 I had had no experience whatsoever with ghosts. Which brings up the next question asked me, "Do you believe in ghosts?" To this question I quote the *Gristogram,* a tabloid newspaper of years gone by. "I know not what the truth may be. I tell the tale that's told to me."

I think of my garage door opening and closing as if by magic. *Abracadabra.* And who, a hundred years ago, or even fifty, would have believed you if you were to describe for them your personal computer—messages that appear on a screen and live cam events happening in real time a half a world away? How about interactive TV that plays games with you—like tennis? And the hundreds of other electronic gadgets that have come into our world to interact with us in such a very short time? I don't understand them myself, but I do know they're for real. So, who is to say, "There's no such thing as ghosts." I think we are on the edge of a new frontier of discovery—the unseen world around us.

Until a few years ago, before television popularized ghost hunting, people kept any paranormal experiences they might have had to themselves for fear of ridicule. Because I keep an open mind and am receptive, many people feel comfortable telling me stories of *their* ghostly experiences. On some ghost walks I *hear* as many stories as I tell. The catalyst for this book was a story was told to me early on in my ghost walk career. I was telling a friend about the history and haunting of Colonial Hall, the big white mansion on Third Avenue built by the Doctors Aldrich in 1904 with the Masonic Lodge, built in 1922, attached to it. "Do you know the Masonic Lodge is haunted as well?" she asked.

"No," I breathed. "Tell me about it."

"I will if you promise not to reveal my name," she replied. "I don't want people thinking I'm nuts." She went on to tell me of the time she was sitting in the upstairs meeting hall when she saw an elderly man dressed in the style of the early 1900's climbing the stairs to the balcony. He paused, looked at her—and dissipated. At the time my friend didn't know the identity of the entity, but I think we do now. She went on to tell me a well-known story of the night the cook was alone in the downstairs kitchen cleaning up after an event. As she was ready to leave the building she saw an elderly man tottering down the hall towards the bathroom. The cook watched and waited for him to come out so she could lock up, but he didn't reappear. Finally, she went to check the bathroom to see if he was okay since it had no exit other than the door she had been watching. Nobody was there. Whatever it was had disappeared into thin air.

The Haunting of the Anoka Masonic Lodge

Lyle Bradley introduced me to John Freeburg during a morning breakfast meeting at Baker's Square a few years ago. John and I hit it off right away. We spent almost the whole time getting to know one another and talking. My ears really perked up when he said he was interested in finding someone to write a book about the hauntings at the Masonic Lodge. I persuaded him that I was qualified by virtue of my ghost tour experience, writing of history columns for the *Anoka Union*, now the *Anoka County Union Herald,* and the time I could devote to the project since I was retired. He agreed and said he would contact the people in the lodge who had had ghostly encounters and let me when he had a list together.

The next time I saw John, he was giving a presentation at the First Congregational Church in Anoka. It was about the Kensington Runestone. Lyle had invited me to attend and I, in turn, invited my sister Gail. We had both had a burning interest in that controversial artifact since high school. Independently of each other we had each read many books on the Runestone over the years and given reports on the subject back in our school days. That morning John introduced us to the work of Scott Wolter, a forensic geologist, who had been hired by the Alexandria Runestone Society in 2000 to test the infamous Stone to determine once and for all whether it was a fraud, as claimed by the "experts," most of whom had never laid eyes on the relic. Or was it authentic? Scott's tests proved conclusively that the Stone and the runes carved on it predated Columbus. He didn't stop there. He went far beyond in his research to find what he believes to be a strong link between the Runestone and the Knights Templar of Europe. Sometime later, Gail and I attended Scott Wolter's talk about the Stone and its meaning which he gave in person at the Masonic Lodge. We bought his book, *The Hooked X*. Wolter's work shows the importance of thinking outside of the box. The same can be said of paranormal phenomena.

John's next invitation was to a presentation by one of the members of the Anoka Freemasons, Josh Fulwider. A police officer by profession, Josh is also a paranormal investigator. He had recently completed an investigation of the Masonic Lodge. I watched in fascination as he gave a PowerPoint presentation of orbs zipping around the screen propelled by some unseen power, heard unexplained knockings and a ghostly voice saying, "Are you working yet?" I was getting antsy about collecting the stories and starting the book.

But no word about it from John.

In October of 2014 I took a six-week community education class at Centennial High School on Paranormal Investigation. It was taught by Dave Schrader, host of Darkness Radio. Dave explained that the purpose of paranormal investigation is to find a logical explanation for extraordinary phenomena. Noises in the walls? Maybe you've got mice—or loose pipes. Orbs in your photos? Maybe your flash picked up dust particles floating in the air. A ghostly image on the print?  Possibly a double exposure.  Door opens mysteriously by itself?  Maybe it needs leveling.  I solved one such mystery in my own home all by myself.  Shortly after my husband died in 2007 the pipes were rattling something fierce. I figured that either he had come back to haunt me or I needed a new furnace.  Sadly, it was my old furnace that had given up the ghost and I needed an expensive new one.  I would have much preferred my husband's ghostly company.

 Dave's paranormal class culminated in January of 2015 when we embarked on a paranormal investigation of the Banfill-Locke House in Fridley.  Built in 1847 and now operating as the Banfill Center for the Arts, this building is the oldest structure in Anoka County. The staff is well-aware aware of the unseen otherworldly occupants they share the space with and it has been proven by previous paranormal investigations to be well-haunted.  With the aid of a Structured Light Sensor (SLS) Camera, we saw plenty evidence of that during the late evening hours.

 It was time to send John an e-mail.

*June Gossler Anderson*

June Gossler Anderson

# Chapters

1. Ghostly Theories 101
11. Doctors Aldrich and Colonial Hall
19. The Ghosts of Colonial Hall
29. Who Are the Freemasons?
39. Haunting Stories from the Masonic Lodge
55. Tools and Technology of Paranormal Investigation
63. Paranormal Investigation of the Masonic Hall
73. A PI and His Theory

June Gossler Anderson

The Haunting of the Anoka Masonic Lodge

*As stated in the Forward to this book I have never, to this point, seen or experienced a ghost except through the aid of technology. Do I "believe" in them? Yes. I definitely believe there is something out there beyond what my five senses are willing to comprehend. I also believe in cell phones, remote controls, televisions, and computers, although I don't understand how any of that works. And I believe that global warming is real and man is an important contributing factor, and the earth is round and revolves around the sun. Why? Because I trust the experts—scientists and engineers who have devoted their careers to researching these concepts.*

*As a researcher myself, when it comes to the metaphysical realm of the paranormal I also rely heavily on the research and experiences of expert and layman alike who tell me their tales and offer explanations. In order to give the reader (and myself) some insight and understanding of the eyewitness accounts of ghostly encounters within the chapters of this book, I have preceded those chapters with background information, historical if you will, about Colonial Mansion and its original owners/occupiers, Doctors Flora and Alanson Aldrich; and Freemasonry, its origin as a stonecutters' guild, its influence in the formation of our country, and its history and importance in Anoka.*

I have titled the first chapter of this book, "Ghostly Theories 101" to try to help explain the phenomena with which we will be dealing and have consulted the works of two experts in the field, Dave Schrader, host of Darkness Radio, and James Van Praagh, producer of the television series, "Ghost Whisperer." While I know Dave personally and have taken a class from him on paranormal investigation, I know Van Praagh only by reputation. He is a psychic and one of those rare people who is a ghost whisperer himself. He has seen full-bodied ghosts since early childhood. Much of the information in this chapter comes from their books, The Other Side, by Dave Schrader and his like-minded friends, and Ghosts Among Us, by James Van Praagh.

Maybe the spirits had a hand in this choice of books. I was just leaving the North Central Branch of the Anoka County Libraries when I happened to see Van Praagh's book beckoning me from the dollar table. Without hesitation I snatched it up. What a bargain

## Ghostly Theories 101

There are many rationales for ghosts, the simplest yet most profound being Anoka Freemason Jordan Stradtman's statement, "Life energy is too powerful to just end."

According to the theory of relativity, mass is converted to energy and energy cannot be destroyed. James Van Praagh goes a step further explaining mass to energy conversion. "Death refers to the end of the physical body. When our spiritual work is done on this earth, our physical bodies shut down and our ghost body exits. The solid, dense energy of our physical body begins to deteriorate. The light, transparent energy body that is an exact replica of the physical body emerges and moves into the spirit worlds." The energy that is now the spirit allows it to move instantaneously from place to place through thought action.

*The Spirit Book* defines a ghost as an "apparition or vision of a spirit of the dead," and the Dictionary.com definition is: 1) The spirit of a dead person, especially one believed to appear in bodily likeness to living persons or to haunt former habitats. 2) The center of spiritual life; the soul. 3) A demon or spirit. 4) A returning or haunting memory or image.

Dave Schrader in his book, *The Other Side*, says ghosts are "Spirits that have yet to move on to the next stage." According to Dave, some other explanations might be "Energy that seems to be trapped," or "Disturbances in time and space." He also has one curious explanation that sounds like it might come directly out of a Harry Potter book. That is the theory of "What's left over." According to Dave's book this theory, common to some of the Eastern religions, says that when we pass on, we move on to the next level, be it heaven, nirvana, or just the next plane of existence. But only the best of who we are moves on—the purest parts of our being. In other words, we might truly have a "split personality" when we die—the "enlightened" parts of us separate and move on, but the rest stays behind—the primitive "animal" aspects of our souls.

Psychics generally agree that there are two classes of spirits, free spirits and earthbound spirits. Free spirits have "passed over" and, as their name implies, are free to come and go at will.

Earthbound spirits are regarded as ghosts and they come in many shapes and sizes. According to Dave Schrader the most common form are vaporous anomalies which show up as mists or vapors, sometimes on film or video.

Sighting a full-bodied apparition is a rare occurrence, and it's even rarer to film or document one.

Those who have seen them describe a ghost that has a full body from top to bottom. Partial-bodied apparitions are just what the name implies. It may be seen as a legless head and torso or maybe as feet and legs tapering to nothingness. Then there are shadow people that can be either full-bodied or partial apparitions. Appearing as two-dimensional shadows, one may get a quick glimpse of them out of the corner of the eye before they disintegrate or disappear.

Earthbound ghosts hang around for a variety of reasons. They may have unfinished business here on earth yet to attend to. That was the ghost's motive in the movie by that name with Patrick Swayze and Demi Moore. He needed to make his killer known. Usually, however, their reasons for staying are more mundane.

Sometimes ghosts don't realize they're dead. This is often the case with those who have died unexpectedly, most often as murder or accident victims. A ghost whisperer friend told me of her mother (also a ghost-whisperer) befriending a planeload of crash victims whose ghosts aimlessly travel together as a group trying to figure out what happened. She welcomed them into her home.

There are those who are afraid to cross over—afraid of what lies in wait for them in the next world. Maybe they have led truly awful lives and fear eternal punishment. More likely they are victims of overzealous preachers who have literally put the fear of god in them so understandably, they don't want to go there.

To this I will add a last category—those who choose to remain. They like it here. They want more sensations of the physical world and, no longer restrained by their physical bodies, they are free to come and go at will. I suspect this might include free spirits as well as earthbound ghosts.

And then there are those with souls so dark that we don't even want to go there. So we won't.

What is their modus operendi? Dave Schrader describes five types of hauntings. An intelligent haunting is when the spirit energy is aware of its surroundings and may deliberately choose to interact with the living by making its presence known. This would account for unexplained knockings, noises, and things being moved. Generally these entities are tied to a specific location.

Transient hauntings are much like intelligent hauntings except these are "drop-in" hauntings rather than being location specific. These earthbound spirits have the ability to roam anywhere on the earth's surface and spend as much or as little time in places that interest them, putting world travel in a whole new dimension.

A third type of haunting would be a residual haunting. Like a recording it repeats over and over again, playing back an event in time. The battlefield at Gettysburg is said to be haunted with those that died there forever re-enacting their roles in scenes played over and over again from that bloody war.

During a writing group I once facilitated, Jack Munday, author of *Justice for Marlys*, described a residual haunting he observed from his kitchen window one morning when he was about to depart for work. Previously, his neighbor woman had been found murdered in her basement and the chief suspect was her husband. On that morning, weeks after her death, Jack happened to see her opening her back door to sweep the dirt out of her kitchen—an act he had witnessed many times before while she was still living. Was it his brain replaying the action or his neighbor's ghost revisiting the scene?

There are the poltergeist hauntings, a term meaning "noisy ghost," where objects are literally being thrown across the room by some unseen force. The jury is out on this one, however. Many researchers attribute this activity to" psychic temper tantrums" caused by the hormonal imbalance of an adolescent teenage girl who is unknowingly causing the problem.

A fifth type of haunting may be a dream visitation, one where the spirit of a deceased friend or relative comes to the living in a dream. Almost all of us have experienced that phenomenon. Was it a dream? Or was it a visit from the spirit world?

Unlike the setting for many a scary tale, ghosts don't hang out at cemeteries, except possibly to attend their own funerals. They need action to generate their energy. Ghosts can be found most any place people are gathered. They especially like places full of life and energy for it energizes them as well. They have been known to haunt theaters and movie sets. Many of them were the former actors and actresses of stage and screen who want to relive and retain their former glory. And of course, who wouldn't want to see the newest Broadway hits or get into the movies for free?

Some newly departed spirits hang out at family gatherings, especially their own funerals where ghost whisperers say they mingle with their families. Nursing homes have their fair share of spirits as well, mostly elderly men waiting for their wives to join them. Some spirits have attached themselves to objects they valued in their earthly life and have accompanied them to museums and antique stores where they now reside.

Bars, sports arenas, emergency rooms, and even dental offices attract spirits for the energy they create, which is often intense and/or negative energy. And police stations are haunted by ghosts with unfinished business, usually dealing with how they ended up dead.

Apparently, ghosts like to travel by public transportation as well as by spirit energy for they can be found haunting bus terminals, subways, airports, and airplanes.

Unhappy ghosts are known to roam the halls of prisons, hospitals, and mental wards. Dave Schrader says that these spirits may represent the raw instincts of their primitive selves of "what's left over." Their enlightened part has already moved on.

I've also read that the halls of Congress are crowded with the ghosts of many self-serving deceased Congressmen bemoaning the fact that they should have done better.

I've never seen a ghost. Have I been cheated of this pleasure? Or have I just ignored what others might have recognized as a paranormal experience and chalked it up to coincidence instead? Maybe I've just been missing the boat and didn't even realize it. But I've met a lot of people who have experienced ghosts. I find they fit roughly into these categories, the first being people who are sensitive to paranormal phenomena, or possibly possess a sixth sense. I think many of the people with stories to tell me are representatives of this group and I think we're just beginning to realize that there are a lot of these people around. In the past they have been reluctant to talk about their experiences for fear of ridicule, but now, they are beginning to come forward and be recognized.

A second category would be psychics and people who see ghosts, like Mary Ann Winkowski, who was both the prototype and consultant for the TV series, *Ghost Whisperer*. On several occasions I have enjoyed lunch with women who see ghosts almost as readily as they see human beings. They claim it is a hereditary or genetic trait. One ghost whisperer said ghosts are around all the time, both from the past and from the future. She said they're just curious, nosy beings. My most recent lunch companion, Patt Corbet, tells of seeing the ghosts of the deceased at their own funerals. She has a camera that takes pictures of orbs and ghostly forms. Maybe it's a magic camera; maybe it displays its amazing ability as a complement to Patt's.

When my mom died the visitors were not in the chapel where her body lay in state. They were in the ante room viewing board pictures from her life and the scrapbooks we had put together for her. When I remarked about this, one guest replied. "This is where her essence is." And perhaps Mom's ghost was there with us as well. Patt says the newly deceased like to mingle with their family at the funeral and at the cemetery before passing over.

A third category would include people with fragile personalities to whom ghosts can prove to be dangerous. One of my friends was possessed by the spirit of an old hag while on a ghost tour in Savannah, Georgia, a notoriously haunted city. She said that, despite a warning, she put her hand on a building known for the evil that lurked inside. Try as she might she wasn't able to free her hand from the building's surface and was taken away by ambulance. She suffered from depression and negativity for over a year, characterizing it as a feeling of oppressive heaviness and lethargy, and along with it, a chronic pain in her side. It was if something was draining all her energy. After ruling out mental and physical reasons, she was put in touch with a psychic known for her ability to recognize and remove the cause of her afflictions. The pain in her side turned out to be the portal through which an evil spirit had entered her body. It disappeared when the psychic was able to exorcise the ghost of an old hag. My friend was planning to go on a paranormal trip to visit the haunted castles of Ireland in September, hosted by Dave Schrader of Darkness Radio. The red flags went up in my mind when

I heard of her intentions. Much to my relief, she realized such an adventure would be far too dangerous for her and canceled out.

Paranormal investigators also realize the danger of "bringing something home with them," and take precautions. These can include surrounding themselves with a white light, saying a prayer of protection, and bringing with them crystals and hematite.

The last category is people like me—people who have never experienced supernatural phenomena. This includes those who declare, "I don't believe in ghosts." Maybe they, like me, have never been in the right situation at the right time. Maybe we're just unobservant and have missed the whole show.

I think there might be another reason for my own lack of paranormal acumen. I had my horoscope read by a professional astrologist. Using my date, time, and place of birth she produced a chart that showed four Taurus signs in the Twelfth House which is the House of Pisces. Taurus is the earth sign, practical and unimaginative. However, the House of Pisces represents everything unseen, mysterious, confused, and mystical which must account for my interest in the occult, psychic phenomena, and psychic energies—all subjects which fascinate me. In and of itself an obsession with this phenomena could be disastrous, but with four Taurus earth signs I'm as firmly grounded as a tree with a deep tap root. I think, while this explains my interest in supernatural phenomena, it also explains what keeps me

June Gossler Anderson

from experiencing it. I have my own built-in protection. Guess I shouldn't complain.

The Haunting of the Anoka Masonic Lodge

## The Doctors Aldrich and Colonial Hall

I wonder if Flora Southard and Alanson Aldrich had any inkling when they married in 1883 that their honeymoon trip to Anoka, Minnesota would last thirty-three years. Although Flora was of an average age when at twenty she married the twenty-eight year old doctor, there was nothing average about her. She was born in Westford, Otsego County, New York in 1863 to S. Wesley Southard, a businessman and "gentleman of the old school." Her mother, Amanda, was the daughter of Isaac Sutherland, a "gentleman of wealth," who was a great believer in education for girls. The three generations, Flora and her brother, her parents, and grandparents all made their home at Sutherland Place, a favorite visiting place for the educated and distinguished of the times.

**Dr. Flora Aldrich**
(Photo courtesy of ACHS)

In this day and age we would say that Flora was home-schooled with her well-educated mother in charge. When Flora was twelve, her mother died. Her education continued, however, at the best local academies under men and women who were specialists in each department. Indeed, at a time when most girls rarely went beyond an eighth grade education, Flora Southard was a well-educated young woman at the time of her marriage to Dr. Alanson George Aldrich, M.D. Upon her marriage, she took up the study of medicine under the tutelage of her doctor-husband.

Dr. Alanson Aldrich, the grandson of David Aldrich, a well-known (at the time) Quaker preacher, was born in 1857 to John Rexford, a day laborer, and Lois Aldrich in Berkshire County, Massachusetts. It's probably due to his maternal grandfather's stature that he took his mother's surname, rather than that of his father. As was often the practice of his day, Alanson Aldrich began his study of medicine under the supervision of a practicing physician before going on to the University of Vermont Medical School and graduating from the College of Physicians and Surgeons in Baltimore, Maryland.

**Dr. Alanson Aldrich**
(Photo courtesy of ACHS)

Doctor Alanson Aldrich had been practicing medicine for three years before he married Miss Flora Southard. Friends had encouraged them to visit the

Northwest (Minnesota) for their honeymoon. In Anoka they encountered the "simple life" they so desired and so they decided to relocate. Dr. Alanson established an eye, ear, nose, and throat practice in both Anoka and Minneapolis and Flora continued her medical studies with her husband; then was admitted to the Minnesota Collage Hospital. Within three years she had graduated from what is now the University of Minnesota Medical School. She followed this up with post graduate work in the New York City Hospital. Then, in 1896 Mr. and Mrs. Doctor left for a year of working and studying in the hospitals of Europe.

Upon their return Mrs. Doctor assisted her husband in his practice and established her own clientele as well. As a woman doctor, Flora's services were gratefully received not only by Anoka women, but by women from the far-flung reaches of other "Northwestern" localities. She was a frequent contributor to medical journals and she published two books. Although Mrs. Doctor had no children of her own, one of her books was practical child raising advice for mothers entitled, *My Child and I*. The other was a book for women with a rather racy title, *A Boudoir Companion for Women,* but it was written to educate women about their own health and hygiene.

By 1904 the Doctors Aldrich had apparently decided they like their adopted city of Anoka well enough to become permanent residents and so they began to build their home on prestigious Third Avenue, a block off Main Street. It was meant to not only serve as their

**Colonial Hall in the early days.**
(Photo courtesy of Anoka County Historical Society)

home, but to house their medical practices as well. The offices were on the north side of the main floor with a separate entrance for patients on that side of the house. Friends used the elegant front door where there is a knocker that bears the name of the house, Colonial Hall.

One of the seventeen rooms of their elegant home was for Dr. Flora's father, S.W. Southard, who, once a successful businessman out East, had lost both his business and inheritance due to dishonest partners. The

**Patients' entrance**
(Photo courtesy of Tom Malone)

doctors had hoped that their companionship would help lift him out of his despair and depression. But that wasn't to be. On one fine day in May, 1906, he managed to kill himself with a shotgun inside Oscar Cutter's barn which was adjacent to Colonial Hall.

Both Drs. Aldrich were advocates of the simple life and enthusiastic students of natural science. Colonial Hall brought Mr. Doctor closer to the pleasures he enjoyed. He kept a private kennel of the finest breeds of hunting dogs, all well trained. In addition to the pleasures of country life he enjoyed good cigars, was a 32 degree Freemason, and was known politically as a "radical democrat and an independent thinker." Among his friends he was known as a "royal good fellow at all times."

Mrs. Doctor was well-respected, and a leader in her community in interests that went beyond medical. She firmly believed in social, political, and economic equality for women at a time when women had second class status. She joined the Women's Suffragettes Movement and marched in Suffragette demonstrations in downtown Minneapolis. She was quoted as saying, "If it is true—and it is true—a woman's moral leverage in the home is an all-important one; then it is true that her moral leverage in the government be an all-important one." And, to promote learning, culture, and refinement in her community, she, along with fifteen other like-minded "women of distinction" established the Philolectian (lovers of learning) Society of Anoka in 1890 which meets still today.

By today's standards both Mr. and Mrs. Doctor died at a relatively young age. Legend gives Mr. Doctor a rather heroic death. With an office in Minneapolis he commuted by trolley. On one subzero (-20 degrees) day in February the trolley was overcrowded so he gallantly gave up his seat to a young woman with a baby and walked the mile to his home where he arrived chilled to the bone and exhausted. In his weakened condition he became ill with pneumonia that, in turn, aggravated a heart condition and within 10 days, on February 19, 1916, he died at the age of 59. His funeral was held in Colonial Hall and conducted by the Scottish Rite Freemasons with hundreds of mourners standing on the lawn outside.

Mrs. Doctor remained active in her organizations and continued seeing patients. Five years after her husband's death, she found herself becoming more and more tired, but nobody thought it a serious matter until, due to heart failure, she died in her bed at Colonial Hall on the morning of March 19, 1921 at the age of 58. Her brother, Lyman, came from the East to take care of her affairs. He sold Colonial Hall to the Freemasons and the furnishings to Eastern Star. The Freemasons built their Lodge Hall and attached it to Colonial Hall. Both buildings share a portion of foundation and are connected by a passageway on the second floor.

Caretakers for the properties lived in Colonial Hall and took care of both buildings and the grounds. In 1971 an agreement between the Lodge and the Anoka

County Historical Society allowed for Colonial Hall to be turned into a museum. For the next 30 years this building housed the collections and offices of ACHS. In 2004 it was leased by the Artique and turned into an antique shop. In 2014 the name was changed to The Big White House.

More information about Colonial Hall and the Doctors Aldrich can be obtained from an excellent booklet written and produced by the Anoka County Historical Society in 2014 from records in the archives of ACHS and personal reminisces of local residents. Titled *Third Avenue Elegance—Colonial Hall and The Doctors Aldrich—A History produced by the Anoka Historical Society*, it is for sale by them.

**Colonial Mansion's transformation into
the present day "Big White House"**
(Photo courtesy of Tom Malone)

## The Haunting of Colonial Hall

The big white mansion located on Third Avenue just off East Main in Anoka was built by a husband and wife team of doctors, Alanson and Flora Aldrich, in 1904 to serve as both their home and medical office. The name on the ornate door knocker gracing the front door of the elegant colonnaded porch identified their dwelling as Colonial Hall. The front door was used by visitors—social friends of the Aldriches. Upon entering the mansion they would find themselves in a large foyer. The formal dining room was to the right with the kitchen behind it. Mr. Doctor's study and library along with their personal rooms were upstairs which was accessible from the foyer by a 90 degree circular staircase winding its way upward. There was another staircase, used mostly by the maids, in the rear of the house.

To the left of the foyer was a beveled glass door, separating the clinic from the doctors' living quarters. Patients entered the clinic through a door on the north side of the house. While Mr. Doctor had an eye, ear, nose, and throat practice in both Minneapolis and

Anoka, Mrs. Doctor specialized in treating women and children in the Anoka area.

Dr. Alanson Aldrich left this earthly realm in 1916. His wife followed him to the grave in 1921. Both were cremated. After the death of Dr. Flora Aldrich, Colonial Hall was sold to the Freemasons who built their lodge on the property the next year, using the upstairs dining room in the house for their formal functions. Anoka Lodge currently has on display Dr. Aldrich's Masonic Sword and his Masonic walking stick.

In 1970 Colonial Hall was leased to the Anoka County Historical Society and it served as their research headquarters and museum for the next thirty years. In 2000 ACHS took advantage of the opportunity to move to the former city library, a move that would provide them with much needed space. Deb Mucklow and her partner, Mary Mestelle, took over the lease, renewed and repurposed the building, and Colonial Hall became the "Artique," a retail business specializing in antiques. By 2013 it had morphed into "The Big White House," housing dealers who specialized in vintage, antiques, and home décor.

During the thirty years from 1970 to 2000 that the Anoka County Historical Society occupied the premises, the staff had noticed unexplained occurrences from time to time—the smell of Mr. Doctor's cigars by the back hallway; or a glimpse of a phantom dog from his kennels running through the building. Items mysteriously disappeared, then reappeared. On one occasion a staffer was going *up* the stairs when she was met by a green mist coming *down* the stairs.

A good yarn of a tale is spun about a display basket filled with balls of yarn through which knitting needles had been poked. Mysteriously, the knitting needles kept jumping out of the yarn balls and landing on the floor. No matter how securely the needles were stuck in the balls the night before closing, they were always lying on the floor by morning when staff entered the building. This happened night after night for a period of time; then stopped of its own accord. The security system detected no motion, yet those darn needles wouldn't stay put. Do ghosts knit?

Maxine Larson served as president of the Anoka County Historical Society in the 1990s, during the time when the organization was housed in Colonial Hall. Of Scottish descent, she had inherited her family's genetic ability to see ghosts, particularly those of their deceased relatives. Maxine said that often, when working late at night in Colonial Hall, she could smell the smoke from Dr. Aldrich's pipe as he moved back and forth between Colonial Hall and the Masonic Lodge through the connecting passage. When her husband was out of town she would often bring her young daughters with to keep her company. The girls were free to roam the premises while their mother worked. In addition to smelling pipe smoke the girls often heard footsteps on the stairs. Although Maxine never actually saw the ghosts, she was aware of the presence of both Dr. Alanson Aldrich and his wife, Dr. Flora Aldrich.

June Gossler Anderson

Prior to establishing the Artique in Colonial Hall, Deb Mucklow and Mary Mestelle were partners in an antique store on the corner of Second and Jackson Street in Anoka. Their business was originally in the building that had housed the Thurston Furniture Store and Mortuary, a not too uncommon marriage of businesses since furniture manufacturers often made coffins and caskets—furniture for this life *and* the afterlife. Many times they went into the funeral business as well. Furniture was sold up front while embalming was done in a room in the back of the store. After a while the two businesses separated. The funeral parlor moved to a new location on Ninth and Main. Thurston Furniture went out of business in the 1990's and Deb and Mary opened an antique store on the premises. Deb said that during their tenancy in the Thurston Building she could sense the presence of many spirits—ghosts if you will—and according to the vibes they gave off, not all of them were friendly.

Unlike their first antique store on Jackson Street, Deb said the new location in Colonial Hall gave off good vibes, creating a happy feeling in the house. During their years of ownership she has had first-hand experiences with the original owners of Colonial Hall, the doctors Flora and Alanson Aldrich, and she feels their presence. When opening up in the morning, both Mary and Deb have heard the sound of footsteps pacing back and forth in the front room at the top of the stairs—the room that was Mr. Doctor's library and study. Sometimes they hear the footsteps come halfway down the stairs, then, as if undecided, turn, and go back up. They feel that it is Mr.

Doctor's ghost moving about. One evening after she had finished her work and locked up Mary was standing by the front door waiting to be picked up. To her surprise she heard a voice in the building call, "Mary!"

"Are you here already?" Mary replied. But nobody was. The building was empty.

Deb says that the ghosts like their presence to be acknowledged. She does this by greeting them in the morning and talking to them during the day. If she is negligent, they have ways to let her know they are there. Deb and two antique dealers once observed the large chandelier just inside the front door swinging back and forth in an arc that almost, but not quite, touched the ceiling. This occurred on a day that the front door was not open to allow a breeze; and since the heat is provided by radiators, forced air heat could not have created an air current. Deb said it was as if to remind her that "you are not alone."

**Deb Mucklow on the stairs in the foyer**
(Photo courtesy of June Anderson)

Most of the ghostly activity seems to occur in the front room parlor and dining room. None has been observed in the part of the house that served as the former patient clinic, although a caretaker for the house died in that room in the 1960s. Mary tells of the day a customer came in and remarked, "I feel an entity here." The entity acknowledged the customer's intuition by proceeding to throw things off a table. Not too very long ago a consignment picture of the Last Supper was hanging in the dining room. Deb was standing about ten feet away from the picture when it came crashing to the floor, although it had been secured by a bolt in the wall. Surprisingly, neither the glass was shattered nor the frame broken by the fall. Again, Deb thought it was the ghosts' way of getting her attention.

Deb tells of a group of junior high girls from the school across the street who liked to stop in the antique store, mainly for thrills since they had heard it was haunted. As they were respectful and well-behaved, they were always welcome. One fine day in March the girls stopped by the store after school and decided it would be fun to take pictures of each other standing at the base of the curving staircase. The got out their cellphones and snapped away. The last picture they took was of the staircase itself, empty—or so they thought until they looked at the picture. Just in front of it and to the side was the misty form of what appeared to be a woman. No one was aware of it when the picture was taken, but there it was.

Much later the mother of the girl who took the picture contacted Deb to tell her she had it and was kind enough to send it to Deb. And here it is.

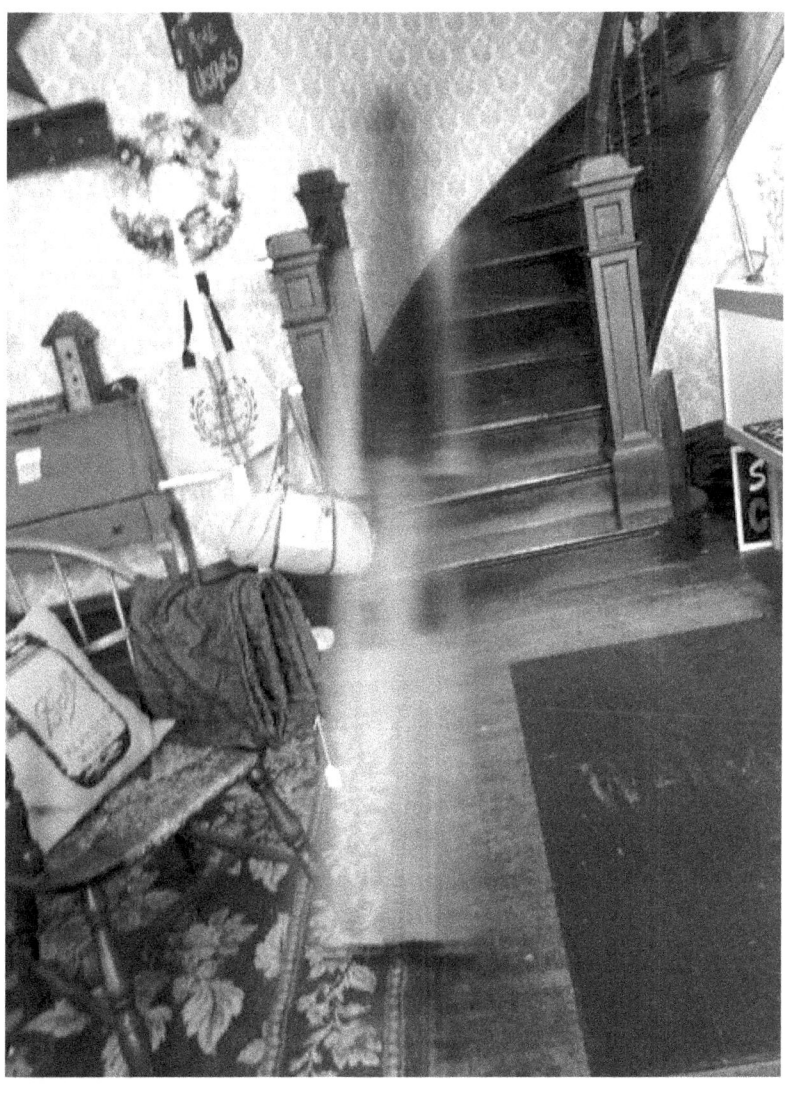

## June Gossler Anderson

Christmas is a special time for the Big White House when it is decked out for the season. One particularly beautiful feature of the house is an archway at the base of the stairway which curves upward to the second floor. It is a popular place to have one's picture taken. In the weeks before Christmas the Anoka merchants hire a Santa Claus to visit the various businesses. He came into the Artique one day during the Christmas holidays of 2013 when a mother and her young son had just finished shopping in the upstairs rooms. When they returned to the main floor, there was Santa. The mother posed her son with the jolly gentleman beneath the festive arch and snapped their picture with her digital camera. The resulting photo showed Santa and the boy—*and* an extra pair of legs standing behind them. The feet were encased in pointed shoes of the type Flora Aldrich would have worn during her days here on earth. Above the shoes the legs tapered into a white, mistiness. No other visible people besides Santa and son had been standing on the staircase when the picture had been taken. The little boy knew instantly who the feet and legs belonged to. "That's the lady who kept blowing in my face when we were upstairs," he insisted. Unfortunately, Deb never did receive a copy of that picture.

Although the ghosts seem to take a lively interest in the goings on in the store, they are mostly quiet when large groups are present. But nighttime tells a different story. The shop has a security system with a motion sensor that works so well that Deb has been roused from her bed to check out a disturbance more than once. One night a baby bat was the intruder setting off the alarm. However, on mornings after a night of undisturbed rest she has arrived at the store to find that furniture has somehow been moved from the wall to the center of the room—without disturbing the sensor!

Shortly after taking up occupancy in November of 2004, the Artique took in a heavy dresser on consignment. It seemed out of place in the front room where they had placed it and apparently the resident entity thought so too, for it attempted to disassemble it. The owners came in one morning to find that the bolts holding the mirror to the back of the dresser had been sheared off and the mirror was lying on the floor—face up in *front* of the dresser. Had the mirror come loose of its own accord it would most likely have fallen off the back, mirror-side up, or if it had fallen forward, the mirror-side would have been down. In either case the mirror probably would have been smashed to smithereens. Instead it had landed nearly intact—in two pieces. A pitcher and bowl that were on the dresser from the night before were totally undisturbed despite the fact that the mirror had fallen forward. The building had been locked and secured for the night with the motion detector activated, so it is highly unlikely that any mortal had had a hand in this.

Deb feels that the good doctors, Flora and Alanson Aldrich, are still hanging around. They are too invested in their home and the community they helped shape to want to leave. Although she thinks these haunted happenings concerning moving and falling objects are the Aldrich's way of getting her attention, they may also be caused by spirits that are attached to the items coming into the antique store to be sold.

Spirits reveal themselves where and when they want. A paranormal investigation conducted at the mansion resulted in an audio of muddy-sounding indistinguishable voices—and a fully charged eight hour battery that was run down after the first half hour of use!

## Who Are the Freemasons?

Freemasonry is the oldest and largest fraternal organization in the world. Its aim is to promote brotherhood and foster morality among its members. Freemasons spend millions of dollars annually for hospitals, homes for widows, orphans, and the aged, relief for people in distress, and scholarships for students. The Shriners, an appendant body to Freemasonry, established and support the Shriners Hospitals for Children, a network of twenty-two medical facilities across North America that treat children with orthopedic conditions, burns, spinal cord injuries, cleft lip and palate. These children receive services in a family-centered environment, regardless of their ability to pay. The Grand Lodge (Freemasons) of Minnesota is the largest contributor of private funding to the cancer research medical center of the University of Minnesota.

If you travel to Europe, you will see historic evidence of Freemasonry in the form of magnificent Gothic cathedrals constructed during the Middle Ages. They were built by skilled stonecutters—craftsmen who were highly valued commodities during that era. Most sought after were the Master Masons who were valued for their knowledge of mathematics, engineering, and drafting ability. Without their expertise, a building project could end up as a pile of rubble. Some cathedrals took well over a hundred years to construct, ensuring employment not only for the Master Mason but for his progeny who served as his apprentice before filling his shoes.

Unlike most people who were tied to the land during that time of feudalism, Masons were free to travel across borders to new sites of employment, hence the name "freemasons." Membership in the Freemason's Guild assured their competency and good character to potential employers and work for themselves. These stoneworkers were the *operative* Masons. Many of the ideas and rituals of Freemasonry originate from this era of cathedral building which, starting in the 1100's saw the blossoming of these mighty Gothic structures.

With the decline of cathedral building in the 1600's, many of the freemasons' organizations became social societies. By the fifteenth century operative lodges in England, Scotland and Ireland began accepting members who had never been stoneworkers. They called these men *speculatives,* or symbolic freemasons. Freemasons base most of their symbols and rituals on the tools and practices of the building profession and to this day, the square and compass, tools used in that profession, serve as the Masonic logo and a reminder of their historic past.

In 1717 four fraternal lodges came together to form the Grand Lodge of England which was the beginning of their organized society. The order spread quickly to other lands, including Colonial America. Among its membership were such famous persons as Benjamin Franklin, Frederik the Great of Prussia, Wolfgang Amadeus Mozart, Voltaire, and George Washington.

Seventeenth century Europe was an age of religious conflict—when an individual caught running afoul of the church could suffer persecution or worse. Freemasons practiced secrecy out of necessity as they searched for religious truth—truth as it existed in all civilizations, including those of a pre-Christian past. They drew upon ancient and occult symbols, from pentagrams to luminescent eyeballs, as codes for ethical development and civic progress. Reactions from church authorities ranged from suspicion to hostility. Thus, European Freemasons had good reason to be discreet.

Although Freemasonry is not a religion, it has brought together men of varied denominations of faith throughout its history. Sharing a common belief in God, Freemasons call Him the "Great (or Grand) Architect of the Universe." A Bible or other holy book is the "furniture" that graces the altar of the meeting lodge.

Freemasons are a diverse group. Since they do not foster any religious, political, or economic creed, they have become one of the world's largest fraternal organizations. As a radical thought movement that emerged from the Reformation, Freemasonry was the first widespread and well-connected organization to embrace religious toleration and liberty—principles that

that fraternity helped spread throughout the American Colonies.

George Washington and other early American Freemasons rejected the oppressive European past in which overarching authority regulated the exchange of ideas. Freemasonry's most radical idea was the encouragement of different faiths within a single nation. This right is embodied in the First Amendment to the Constitution which grants us freedom *of* and *from* religion.

Twenty-eight of the forty signers of the Constitution were Freemasons or possible Freemasons. In addition to George Washington the majority of the twenty greatest men of the American Revolution were also Freemasons or had close connections to Freemasons. These included Ethan Allen, Edmund Burke, John Claypoole, William Daws, Benjamin Franklin, John Hancock, Thomas Jefferson, John Paul Jones, Robert Livingston, James Madison, Paul Revere, Colonel Benjamin Tupper, and Daniel Webster.

It's interesting to note that Lafayette, French military liaison to the Colonies whose aid was essential to the winning of the Revolutionary War, was a Freemason and, ironically, the majority of the commanders of the Continental Army and most of Washington's generals were Freemasons as well.

Many of the symbols and ideals of Freemasonry live on in the capital city of our nation.

## Freemasonry Comes to Anoka

According to Anoka Lodge #30 historian, John Freeburg, "Our lodge began with a group of men who were in pursuit of that high ideal which all masons share—to seek that light which can only shine from within and which illuminates the path which leads us to becoming better than we were."

(Photo courtesy of Tom Malone)

Many of the early arrivals to Anoka came from the New England States where there was already a tradition of Freemasonry. They established their Lodge on October 25, 1859, the year after Minnesota became a state. Like their Colonial counterparts, the Lodge's early members included many of the movers and shakers of their adopted city. Among them was Dwight Woodbury, a charter member of that first lodge. Hailing originally from Massachusetts, he came to Anoka in 1855 where he proceeded to buy the water rights and large tracts of land in St. Francis, as well as Anoka, on which to build his sawmills. Woodbury is also credited with the platting of both those cities. He was elected to the Minnesota House of Representative in 1863, and the home he bought on Ferry Street in 1860 served as the scene for social and political gatherings as well as a safe haven for people fleeing to Anoka for fear of Indian attacks during the Dakota Indian War in 1862. That historic house still stands, now the home of the Mad Hatter Restaurant.

Other citizens of note over the years who also served as Worshipful Masters of the Lodge included: Albert Woodbury, son of Dwight Woodbury, who raised a regiment to fight in the Civil War and lost his life in the Battle of Chickamauga; William Cundy, a lumberman, who joined the Minnesota First with Aaron Greenwald, the first volunteer in the Union Army; Josiah Clark, first probate judge of Anoka County and principal musician with the Minnesota Eighth Regiment during the Civil War; and Heman (not Herman) Ticknor, who was the leading druggist in Anoka for 35 years. Heman married Anna Greenwald, widow of Aaron Greenwald who was mortally wounded at Gettysburg, and built for her and Aaron's two sons, a house known as the Ticknor Mansion on Third Avenue which is now a lovely bed and breakfast.

Oscar Cutter, another prominent citizen of Anoka, was a Worshipful Master as well, setting a record by serving five terms in that office. According to Goodrich's *History of Anoka County,* "He was a man of extraordinary popularity and served in some public capacity almost his whole life. He was county auditor for several terms, judge of probate, deputy county treasurer, city clerk, alderman, mayor, city assessor, treasurer of the school board, chief of the fire department, and Secretary of the Minnesota State Senate in 1887 and 1889."

Charlie Horn, founder of Federal Cartridge in Anoka, was another prominent Anokan who was a Freemason. Although not of the Anoka Blue (first three degrees) Lodge, Charlie belonged to a lodge in Minneapolis, was a member of the Scottish Rite, and also a Shriner.

Not much is known of the early days of the Anoka Lodge, for its original records, along with all of its possessions, were destroyed during the Great Fire of 1884 which also wiped out most of the business district of Anoka. Existing records date from September of that year when, a month after the fire, the Anoka Freemasons resumed their meetings at the Merchant's Hotel where they continued to meet until 1919 when they moved to Workman Hall at the corner of First Avenue and Main Street. In 1922 the Freemasons laid the cornerstone for their present building on land purchased from the Aldrich estate after the death of Dr. Flora Aldrich the previous year. Her husband, Doctor Alanson Aldrich, had died in 1916. Although Mr. Doctor had never served as Worshipful Master he had been very active in the Anoka Lodge and other Masonic organization such as the Scottish and York Rites.

## June Gossler Anderson

Many of these early records documented charitable activities such as giving financial assistance to the wives, widows, mothers, sisters, and children of Lodge members in need. In some cases, the Lodge was their sole support. In 1894 the Lodge appropriated $15.00 for the relief of victims of the Hinckley Fire. The Freemasons took part in the cornerstone laying ceremony of the new Anoka High School in 1904 which later became Sandburg Middle School and during the Great Depression many Lodge members personally extended financial aid to members and non-members alike.

In 1981 the Anoka Lodge decided to give a scholarship to graduating seniors from the Anoka-Hennepin school district. The scholarship program was soon extended to include deserving youth throughout Anoka County. During the late 1980s and early 1990s Anoka Lodge #30 sponsored the Coon Rapids Sno-Cruisers' snowmobile club in many fund-raising snowmobile rides which raised tens of thousands of dollars for the Minnesota Masonic Cancer Center.

As an active part of the community, the Anoka Lodge takes part in many of its festive occasions. Since 1983 they have hosted a Christmas party for children complete with games, songs and treats; each year they have a float in the annual Anoka Halloween Parade; and during Anoka County Fair week in late July they have an information booth on the fair grounds.

In his brief history of the Masonic Lodge, Lodge Historian, John Freeburg, adds an interesting insight.

"Before February 26, 1926 the stated Lodge meetings were held on the Saturday night that was closest to the full moon. This was a common practice for lodges at the time. Lodges meeting under these circumstances were known as "Moon Lodges." The reason for meeting near the time of the full moon was to take advantage of its light for traveling at night."

Related organizations to the Freemasons include the Order of DeMolay (boys), Order of Eastern Star (women), Job's Daughters (girls), Knights Templars, and Shriners. The Lodge also sponsors a Cub Scout and Boy Scout troop.

**East wall of the meeting room in the Anoka Masonic Lodge**
(Photo courtesy of Tom Malone)

**West wall and balcony of the meeting room in the Anoka Masonic Lodge**
(Photo courtesy of Tom Malone)

The Haunting of the Anoka Masonic Lodge

## Haunting Stories from the Masonic Lodge

In 1985 Al Nemchik was the Worshipful Master of Anoka Masonic Lodge. The Lodge building is connected to Colonial Hall which the Freemasons have owned for many years. In 1985 the Lodge office was upstairs, across from the Lodge meeting room. That room is now used by Job's Daughters. Although it's no longer accessible, there was and still is a door in that room that is common to both buildings. On the other side of the door is Colonial Hall, the one-time residence and clinic of the Doctors Aldrich—Alanson and Flora. The good doctors died in 1916 and 1921 respectively.

Al was tending to some Lodge business at about midnight one night when he distinctly heard the front entrance door slam shut. He wondered who would be on the premises at that late hour so he went to the top landing and called out. Nobody answered and the lights downstairs were off. He went downstairs to see who had come in and was standing in the dark. Nobody was there. He checked the door and it was locked, just as he had left it.

Al went back to work in what was then the office. From the other side of the disabled common door he heard a dog bark twice and then smelled the distinct odor of either a pipe or cigar. Al found this very unsettling as he knew Dr. Alanson Aldrich had been an avid hunter and had kept hunting dogs. He got the message and left. As Al was sober and clear-headed at the time this happened, there was no mistaking what he had heard and smelled that night.

In 2010 when Al was a trustee the Freemasons installed an elevator in the building. Dave Emery, also a trustee, and Al were working on various projects one Saturday and had taken a break in the basement club room. As they talked they heard a distinct sound that they both identified as a shovel scraping dirt on a hard surface. Looking at one another they wondered who could be working on the elevator construction. Immediately, they went outside to take a look. There was neither person nor vehicle in the lot save their own. They concluded that maybe their benevolent spirit was getting anxious to see the project completed and just wanted to help it along.

Several years ago when Harold Kroeger was Lodge secretary, a young college lad was hired to come in and help the Lodge out with janitorial duties. Being a typical youth he enjoyed music, really loud music. He would turn his radio up full volume and place it in various locations, depending on where he was working. After the young man had been working for the Lodge for a while, Al and Harold became aware that he was having some unsettling experiences. While he was going about his duties, somehow the volume on his radio kept getting turned down, even turned off completely. Both Al and Harold thought it was pretty comical, but apparently it wasn't so funny to the young man. One day he had the radio in the kitchen and was working in the rear of the Lodge. After several incremental turn downs he went to turn the sound back up. Walking into the kitchen he found several boxes which had been neatly stacked, thrown all around. That was the last straw! He grabbed his radio, and the last thing the two Freemasons heard was, "I'm never coming back! Send me my check." And once again, silence prevailed.

In the fall of 1987 when Steve Bernu was Worshipful Master, he and Tim Hunter (PM 1988) were upstairs in the Lodge Room rehearsing a lecture for incoming initiates. The room was lit by the large globe lights widely in use at the time. The glass globes were attached to the hanging light fixture by three screws. As Steve and Tim rehearsed in the otherwise quiet room they heard the distinctive sound of a screw turning—metal grating against glass. Then a second screw, followed by a third screw. Somehow, the three screws securing globe to fixture had loosened themselves one after another and, as Steve and Tim watched in shaken surprise, the glass globe smashed to the floor. No explanation. It just happened.

Next to the Lodge Room is the Preparation Room where new Masonic candidates await their initiation rites. After a meeting one hot summer night of the same year Steve was the last one to leave the building and as such, he was responsible for locking up and securing it. Having discharged his duties, he got in his car to leave. Looking back at the Masonic Hall Steve saw that the light was on in the Prep Room. So he got out of his car, climbed the stairs, and turned off the light. Mission accomplished, Steve went back to the parking lot, got in his car, glanced at the building—and again saw the light in the Prep Room glowing brightly. He got out of his car again, re-entered the building, made his way upstairs, and once again turned off the light. But this time he decided that he'd better check the whole building, including the lower level.

There is a large full-length antique mirror at the bottom of the basement steps. When coming down the stairs you can only see the lower half of your reflection because the ceiling above you blocks out the top half. As Steve descended the stairs that evening he heard footsteps behind him. In the mirror before him he could see his own reflection—as well as that of another! To the rear and left of his image was a pair of black trousers clad in black shoes coming down the

## The Haunting of the Anoka Masonic Lodge

stairs right behind him! Quickly, he whirled about only to find nobody there!

Steve made a bee-line for the door. Locking it as he left, he got back in his car only to see that the light in the Prep Room was on again! Totally exasperated, he got out of his car, opened the door to the Masonic Lodge, and called to the unseen intruder, "Turn the damn light off yourself!" And the light went out.

Steve told his story to another Freemason, Clarence Groth (PM 1957). Clarence's comment? "The same thing happened to me in 1957."

About 2006 or 2007 Dave Emery was sitting in a meeting being held in the Lodge Room of the Masonic Hall. His attention was diverted from the events on the floor to one occurring on the ceiling overhead. The room was illuminated by six hanging globe lights. Five of them hung perfectly straight and still, but he noticed the one in the northwest corner of the room swaying gently back and forth of its own accord. As he watched, the globe began to swing more and more vigorously, reaching an arc of about six inches. There were no air currents to precipitate the swinging and none of the other five lights were affected; they remained perfectly still while the

sixth one seemed to be having a party of its own. It continued swinging back and forth for several minutes before it abruptly stopped. One of the woman attendees looked at Dave and said, "I didn't see anything," to which Dave replied, "Neither did I."

Late one evening 'round about 2009, Jordan Stradtman (PM 2003) was alone in the Lodge Room getting ready for an event to be held the next day. Finished with his duties upstairs he turned off the lights, closed the door, and went downstairs to the kitchen. While in the kitchen he heard stuff going on upstairs. Up he went to check on the source of the disturbance. It was coming from a small radio sitting on the sign-in desk that was for use only in case of weather emergencies. Jordan checked the Lodge Room, but no one that he could see was there. Turning off the radio he went back down to the kitchen. No sooner had he gotten there then the radio somehow turned itself back on. Again Jordan went back upstairs to check. No one was there. He turned the radio off and returned to the kitchen. When the radio turned itself back on for a third time, Jordan decided it was time to leave.

Later, when relating his experience to his fellow Masons they joked, "The doctor must have wanted to listen to the radio."

Dave Lundquist is a Freemason and his wife, Garland, belongs to the Order of Eastern Star. They were caretakers for the Masonic Lodge from 2005 to 2013. Although they never *saw* anything, they *were* witness to unexplained happenings. By this time the globe lights in the Lodge Room had been updated to chandelier style lights, but like the lights of old, the new ones were suspended from the ceiling on chains. On many occasions the Lundquists observed some or all of them swinging from their chains, sometimes all together, sometimes independently of one another—and in different directions. Sometimes the ceiling fans swayed from side to side as well. Dave tells of a particular light fixture that kept turning itself on and off for no apparent reason. Nothing was wrong with the fixture and replacing the bulb did not fix the problem. It still turned on and off of its own free will—or the will of something else.

Garland tells of unexplained temperature differentials in the lower level where the ladies of the Eastern Star held their meetings. Sometimes it would be very cold; then inexplicably become hot. The ladies were uneasy using the downstairs bathrooms which were located near the side of the building where it shares a common foundation with the Big White House (formerly Colonial Hall). The bathrooms were unheated and drafty and the space near the floor was much colder than that at head level. Garland said that there seemed to be a presence there.

The Lundquists' son, Mark, is a plumber. Although not a member of the lodge he often stopped by at his parents' request to take care of minor plumbing problems. Mark tells of the time he was called upon to make a repair on the tank of one of the toilets in the basement. Sitting backwards on the stool he took the lid off the tank to examine its innards. The door to the right of him was open. As he happened to glance towards it, he

saw a pair of shoes walking by. They were big and black and translucent—a nicely polished pair of dress shoes with a buckle on top. In amazement he watched the shoes walk towards a storage closet near the bathrooms and disappear. Later he called his mom and jokingly asked her, "Do you have a ghost in the house." To his surprise, she answered, "Well, yes. It must have been the doctor."

Garland said that on the days she came to clean she would open the front door of the Masonic Lodge and carefully shut it behind her. On occasion the door would open again of its own accord; then close, as if someone had entered the building after her. But it was no one that she could see. Garland, along with many others, felt it was the ghost of Dr. Alanson Aldrich. She got in the habit of calling out "Hi Doc," when opening the door; then would add, "I'm here to clean." or "We're here to set up tables," etc. She felt that the good doctor liked to know what was going on.

The kitchen and eating area of the Masonic Hall occupy the lower level. A refrigerator and freezer are located in the back hall. About three years ago, in 2012, senior warden Paul Agustin stopped by with his six-year old son to put some food in the old chest style freezer. No one else was in the building at the time. As he stashed the food Paul noticed a drop in temperature, not attributable to the cold given off by the freezer. His son, who was amusing himself close by, asked, "Who's that, Dad?"

"Who?" Paul asked.

"That guy who just bumped into me and went upstairs," replied the boy. Although his son was in plain sight all the time, Paul hadn't seen anyone else.

Steward Josh Fulwider, and Jeremy Hill, junior steward, were in the kitchen preparing dinner for their fellow Masons on the night of February 3rd 2015. It was

**Josh Fulwider in the kitchen.**
(Photo courtesy of Tom Malone)

the first Wednesday of the month, their meeting night which was always preceded by a meal. Jeremy was cooking up hash browns on the grill and Josh had the burners on the stove going full blast as he fried up the bacon and eggs to go with the hash browns. It was wickedly hot in the kitchen and both men were sweating bullets.

Suddenly, the temperature dropped. Josh estimated that it was a full twenty degrees change between the stove and the rest of the area. He and Jeremy went from sweating hot to bone-cold chilled. At that instance Josh turned and saw a figure in the pass-through window. He described it as a fuzzy blackness that blocked out the light. He could make out its head, shoulders, and the rest of the body to mid torso. When the figure realized that Josh and Jeremy could see it, it quickly darted away.

"Did you see that!" Josh exclaimed.
"Ain't no joke," Jeremy replied in his southern drawl.
"Come visit. Say hi," said Josh as he tried to coax the entity into making a return appearance.

About half an hour later Jeremy was moving to go around the preparation table when he saw something. There it was again! Walking in front of the pop machine.

The entity is a frequent visitor. Josh says he has seen it at least a half dozen times. It's a watcher—curious and observing, not interacting in any way. It appears to be something with both intelligence and intent.

Josh frequently observes shadows moving along the lower level hallway between the common foundation wall shared by both Colonial Mansion and the Masonic Lodge to the opposite side of the basement. He thinks that this is a residual haunting; an apparition that is not a spirit, but a recording or playback of a recurring event.

George Atwood was both a member of the Masonic Lodge and past president of the Anoka County Historical Society. A carpenter by trade and a bachelor by choice he lived well into his 90s. During his lifetime he was a passionate member of the ACHS, then housed in Colonial Hall. He joined the board in the late 70s and served as treasurer before assuming the position of president. Despite his auspicious position, he dressed casually, often wearing overalls and a red plaid shirt, a mode of dress well suited to a carpenter. It is thought by many that even in death he still retains his attachment to both organizations. Some people claim to have seen an entity in a red plaid shirt sitting in the balcony; others have observed it in other locations.

After finishing with their business at the Masonic Hall one evening in 1991, Larry Jensen who was Worshipful Master at the time, and his brother-in-law, Ray Hinkley (PM 1992 ) were sitting and chatting in

Ray's pickup in the parking lot on the north end of the building. From the truck they had a clear view of the long window in the building that looked down into the lower level. After about ten minutes, by the glow cast by the security lights, they saw the figure of a black-haired man dressed in a red and black plaid shirt, the kind that might have been worn by a hunter in the 40's or 50's. They were puzzled, thinking that somebody was still in the lodge. As they watched he made his way from the emergency exit on the south side of the building to the north side that led to the stairway leading to the outside of the building. The men got out of the truck and unlocked the door thinking they had locked someone inside the building but they couldn't find the guy. They figured he must have let himself out through the emergency door in the rear and thought nothing more of it.

    About two weeks later they mentioned the incident to several of the other Masons and Order of the Eastern Star members. "That's the ghost!" one responded. Unknown to Larry and Ray, the man in the red plaid shirt was a frequent visitor to the lodge. But he was not of this world.


    In 2010 when Kristen was eleven she attended a Job's Daughter sleepover in the Masonic Lodge along with about fifteen other girls and three or four female chaperones. The girls spent the early part of the evening partying in the lower level playing board games and Twister, dancing with the DJ's, and feasting on pizza and ice cream. Then they went upstairs to the Lodge Room. After watching a movie they blew up their air mattresses, spread out their sleeping bags, and fell asleep—all but Kristen and her friend who lay awake talking quietly to each other. They were just about to doze off when they saw something that jolted them wide awake. A form silently entered the room through the door on the east side to the rear of the room. By the dim light they could make out a figure dressed like a farmer and wearing a red plaid shirt. They knew it was a ghost because there were no men in the lodge with them that night and they had heard their fathers describe the looks of what they were now seeing. Not wanting the ghostly visitor to see

**West wall of Lodge meeting room showing doors on either side and stairways leading up to balcony. That's Josh, not a ghost.**
(Photo courtesy of Tom Malone)

them, the girls froze. As they watched, the apparition stopped and stood facing the west wall, then walked over to the door on that side of the room and left. At first Kirsten thought she was in a dream. Realizing it wasn't one freaked her out. She was afraid to sleep because she was scared he would come back out. She told her friend they should wake everyone up and tell them what they had just seen. Her friend calmed her down saying, "We will tomorrow morning." And so they did.

A year later in 2011 Kristen was attending a Job's Daughter's meeting in the Lodge Room. She had two responsibilities at that meeting. One was as a guide for the other girls and the second was to make sure the left-hand side door remained closed. She was stationed near the assigned door when it popped open of its own accord. Kristen got up and closed the door. Hearing it click she returned to her seat. No sooner was she seated than the door popped open again. Nobody was there. Again she got up to close it, making sure the latch clicked in place. Then it happened over and over and over again. After closing it for the fifth time Kristen gave up and asked one of the fathers in the room to shut the door. He had no better luck for despite his best efforts the door continued to pop open. Evidently, somebody or something wanted in. Could the party crasher have been George Atwell?

Kristen says that she always feels a presence when she is in the building—an uncomfortable presence, like someone is walking close behind her. She tells of the time she was in the building with her father tending to the pop machine on the lower level. Although they were the only ones there they could hear footsteps of someone moving around—not upstairs or downstairs where they were; the sound seemed to come from a level in-between. However, there is no middle level in the Masonic Lodge.

Kristen tells of a friend who went upstairs by herself. She freaked out when she saw a white blur in the hallway just outside the Lodge Room.

Like pieces of a jigsaw puzzle each of these stories is interesting in and of itself, but it's when you begin to assemble them that you start to see the whole picture. In Colonial Hall, now the Big White House, there seem to be two primary ghosts, the main suspects being Dr. Alanson Aldrich and Dr. Flora Aldrich. The two prime suspects in the Masonic Lodge haunting are Dr. Alanson Aldrich and George Atwood, both Freemasons who seem to be still enjoying the companionship of their brother Freemasons.

But, there could be more.

**Ghost Hunting Paraphernalia: Left- MelMeter, measures temperature and electromagnetic field; Middle- REM Pod detects motion and energy disturbances. Emits a beep when the beam is interrupted. Right- Electro Static Pod.**
(Photo courtesy Tom Malone)

## Technology and Tools for Paranormal Research and Investigations

*According to Dave Estuestabell of the Anoka Paranormal Society, "Paranormal research is the permutation of science, history, spirituality, and logic."*

Throughout history people of nearly every culture have believed in the existence of spirits, or ghosts and along with it a strong belief in the afterlife. (After all, isn't that what religion is all about?) They have engaged in various ways to make contact with the dead. Shamans have and still do serve that purpose in many societies. In some societies mediums and psychics claim to have the "gift." Paranormal investigators, often known as "PIs," have taken up the call in more modern time but their mission is two-fold. Believe it or not their primary purpose is to debunk—to find logical explanations for unusual happenings before considering the paranormal aspects of the phenomena. They explore the world of the metaphysical that occupies a niche somewhere between scientific proofs that are demonstrably repeatable and religion which relies strongly on faith and belief.

By human standards ghosts are not predictable. Inhabitants of the world between the secular and the religious—the metaphysical world—they seem to operate by their own set of rules. Theirs are the laws, not of physics or gravity, but of trans-physical science that I believe we are on the verge of discovering through new cutting-edge technology in the field of paranormal investigation.

Albert Einstein theorized that there are eleven dimensions. We living beings live in two of them. What about the rest? Are there inter-dimensional beings occupying the other nine? Would one of these dimensions be where ghosts and spirits hang out? How do we make contact with them, and vice-versa? Paranormal investigators are trying their best and they have a whole toolbox of sophisticated devices to help them out. Among the most commonly used are:

**Electromagnetic Field Meter (EMF)**

The discovery of electricity and its resulting inventions has opened a pathway of sorts to the spirit world. Spirits seem to feed off this energy, and in turn, devices using electricity are making possible elementary forms of communication with these unseen entities. EMF (Electromagnetic Field Meters) are used to measure electromagnetic fields. Since we are surrounded by an electromagnetic field, the detector detects ordinary things, such as nails in a stud. Anomalies are just a by-product. Many amateur ghost hunters use EMF detectors that are of the household variety. EMFs are used extensively by ghost hunting groups that believe the presence of EMF spikes on the meter that can't be identified as "hot spots" in the wiring are the result of a ghost trying to manifest itself or communicate using the electrical energy in the room.

## Thermometers

Ghosts also tend to feed off of heat energy causing the temperature to drop. These temperature drops can indicate the presence of a ghost manifesting and drawing temperature from a specific area.

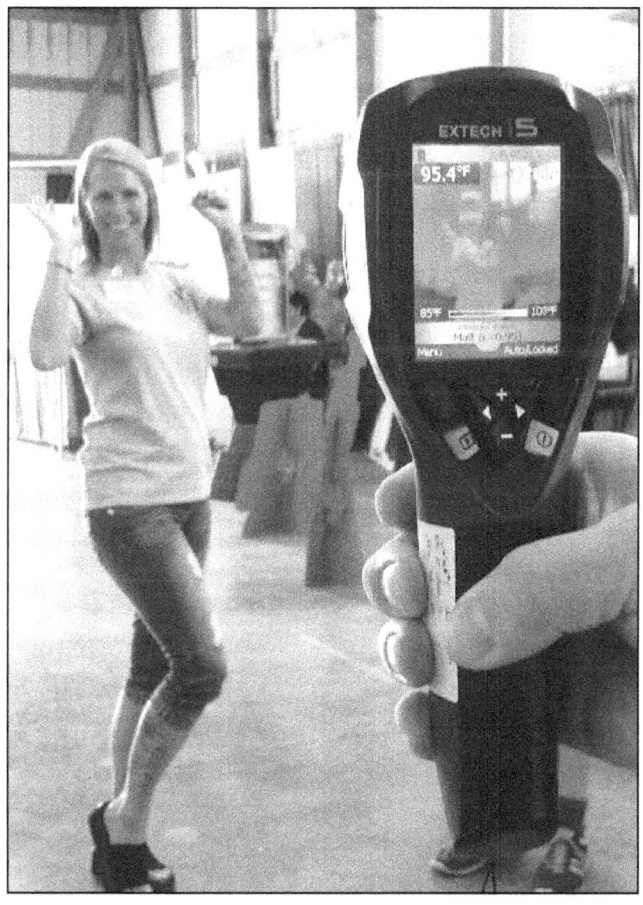

**Flir Extech 15 Thermal Camera. Body heat of the subject registers in color (shades of red)**
(Photo courtesy June Anderson)

## Cameras

Since George Eastman invented the Kodak camera in 1888 people have been photographing ghosts, both accidently and on purpose. Sometimes a spirit turns up spontaneously in a picture; sometimes it happens with the help of the photographer making a double exposure or using some other trick of photography. Modern digital cameras are great for photographing what isn't there—like a ghost, but sophisticated apps make it possible for a person to produce his or her own ghost on a picture as well.

Images most often captured by cameras are orbs, sometimes knows as "spirit lights." Orbs are thought to be intelligent light sources. However, there can be many non-paranormal reasons for orbs to show up in pictures. Most common is the presence of dust particles picked up by the flash of the camera. The air is full of dust particles. Just observe a ray of sunshine beaming in the window. In a still picture authentic orbs are more likely to be those that are partially obscured by distant objects such as trees and rocks.

The origin of orbs captured on video is easy to identify by observing how they are moving. Dust particles will float, usually leisurely—up, down, or sideways—depending on drafts. Intelligent orbs zip around with a purpose, usually fast and erratic.

Camcorders used in paranormal investigations are set up to continuously record in an attempt to capture images in specific locations and they can be fitted with a night vision scope. Unlike a film camera, a digital camera can take many pictures in a very short period of time increasing the odds of taking an accurate, identifiable ghost picture. Thermal imaging cameras or infra-red devices will pick up any sources of heat and capture those images.

**Digital Voice Recorders**

Often referred to as "EVPs," Electronic Voice Phenomena, Digital Voice Recorders can pick up voices that the human ear can't initially hear. Often an ordinary tape recorder will do the job. Older tape recorders usually work better than the newer "improved" models that filter out extraneous noise, the very noises that PIs want to capture.

Sometimes ghost voices are picked up by radio on frequencies found between broadcasting stations, suggesting that they might have their own frequency. The challenge for sound engineers is to find the right frequency for these inaudible voices.

Since paranormal entities are notorious consumers of energy, extra batteries are a must. They may not put in an appearance at an investigation, but they can still suck the life out of a PIs' batteries as many a paranormal investigator has discovered much to his/her chagrin.

**Latest technology in ghost hunting equipment**

On October 10, 2014 during a class on paranormal investigation, Dave Schrader, our instructor and host of

Darkness Radio, brought in Bill Chappel via Skype. Bill lives in Colorado. He is an engineer who invents sound and visual devices to record "extracurricular" activity of unexplained origin ie. Paranormal Technology. Bill is associated with the TV show, "Ghost Adventures" where his state-of-the art equipment is used on their investigations

Two of Bill's cutting edge sensing devices are the Ovilus, a device that is used to record sound, namely voices, and a Structured Light Sensor (SLS) camera which photographs creatures unseen by the naked eye. Bill feels that possibly within five years there will be a scientific breakthrough in spirit communication and he is hard at work making that happen.

The Ovilus is a major step forward in Instrumental Trans Communication (ITC) devices. ITCs are devices that use an electronic or mechanical means to allow spirit communication with real human voices by converting environmental readings into words.

**Structured Light Sensor Camera**

Based on the technology of the Kinect camera, the SLS is a scanning camera that will capture and understand the environment. The connected PC based tablet collects all the data into one central point for simple viewing and recording. One single screen shows all the data: Temperature, Imaging, Audio Range, Distance, Light Levels and Visualized Object Scanning. It is not only portable and mountable but also a self-contained device. The portable SLS is about the same size and shape as an iPad with a handle for gripping on the bottom and a screen for viewing on top. The camera itself is on the leading edge. It works on the same principle as sonar imaging, but instead of shooting sound waves through water it shoots light rays though air. Like sonar, when these beams of light are interrupted by something in their path, they form an image.

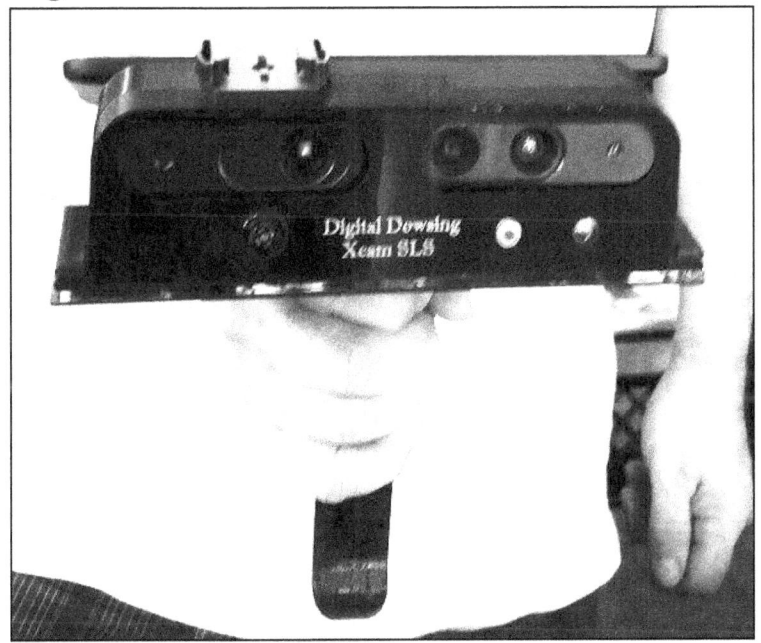

**Portable Structured Light Sensor Camera showing camera eye on the front edge.**
(Photo courtesy June Anderson)

The SLS camera works the same way as the Kinect camera mounted on your television that reads your body motions when you play interactive electronic games with it. The camera requires 18 points of contact to identify an image which shows up on the screen as a glowing stick figure with lines connecting the dots. Upon contact, a panel shows green, blue, or red along with the words "anomaly sighted" and pretty soon the stick figure hops into view. With a click of the "record" button its movement can be recorded for future viewing as well. (Reminds me of the new rage in Halloween costumes— LED lights outlining the figure wearing it.)

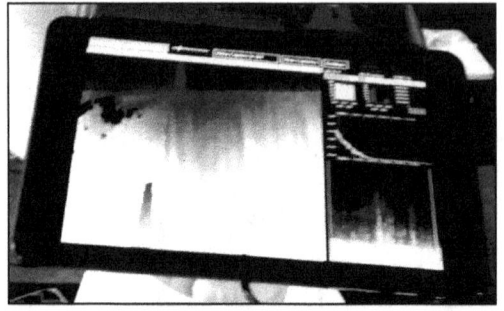

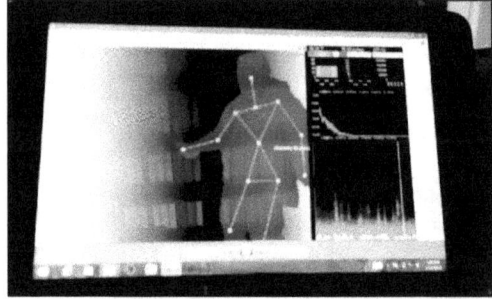

**Viewing screens of the SLS Camera. Top screen registers no activity. Bottom screen shows mapping of a human form. An unseen entity would show up as just the dots and connecting lines.**

(Photo courtesy June Anderson)

But, no matter how sophisticated and cutting edge their equipment may be, as many a paranormal investigator has discovered, ghosts don't do command performances. They come and go at will and make their presence known when and if they feel like it. They are spontaneous creatures, showing up when it suits their purpose. Ghosts operate by their own set of rules.

## Paranormal Investigation of the Masonic Lodge

**Part One**

  John Freeburg, knowing of my interest in paranormal phenomenon, invited me to dine with the Freemasons the evening of May 7, 2014. After dinner Josh Fulwider, one of their own and also a paranormal investigator, would be making a presentation of his findings during a paranormal investigation of the lodge earlier in the year. I sat spellbound listening to Josh's PowerPoint presentation. It showed orbs that definitely had an energy all their own, darting hither and thither. There were knocking sounds as if in response to a question posed by the investigator, and a disembodied voice captured on an EVP saying, "Are you working yet?" This was significant. When Freemasons are in a business meeting or in an initiation meeting for new members they consider themselves to be "at labor" or "working." The phrase was identified as coming from George Atwood, a deceased member of the Masonic Lodge who was basically asking, "Is the Lodge conducting a meeting?"

I was hooked on ghost hunting. In the fall of the year I signed up for a six-week class on paranormal investigation offered by Dave Schrader, host of Darkness Radio, through Centennial School District Community Education. The October classes culminated in January with an investigation of the Banfill-Locke House, now an art center in Fridley, Minnesota. And we saw ghosts! The place was loaded with them and we could see them in real time on the viewing screens of the two SLS cameras Dave and another paranormal investigator, Kevin Swanson, had brought with them. I have included a description of that haunting in the Afterward of this book.

Then I had a thought. Wouldn't it be great if Kevin and his SLS Camera and Josh, and I, as an observer, got together for another paranormal investigation of the Masonic Lodge? Oh, the things we would see! Kevin and Josh were agreeable and so agreed to meet on June 27th 2015 to become acquainted

Three intrepid ghost hunters about to embark on a paranormal investigation of the Anoka Masonic Lodge. Left to right: Josh Fulwider, PI, June Anderson, author, Kevin Swanson, PI.
(Photo courtesy Tom Malone)

with the ghosts that have made the Lodge their earthly home.

With Josh's permission I invited my sister, Laurie Malone, and her husband, Tom, to join us for the early part of the evening. Tom is a photographer and I wanted him to take some pictures of the building, inside and out; of the investigators—Josh, Kevin, and me; and of some of the equipment we would be using. The DeMolay Chapter which had met earlier had left by 7:00 and the building was now quiet and empty.

We entered the Masonic Hall and went downstairs to the kitchen. We had barely gotten settled when Tom exclaimed, "What was that!" and described a shadow he had seen beyond the pass-through moving down the hallway. This was not the first ghost Tom has encountered in his lifetime. He has the gift; some say it's genetic. We waited for the entity to appear again, but nothing happened and Tom proceeded to photograph the ghost hunting paraphernalia we would be using.

**Door opening to hallway beyond kitchen, through which a shadow is often seen making it's way along the passage.**

**Looking through the kitchen into the dining room beyond from the hallway.**
(Photo courtesy of Tom Malone)

Meanwhile, Josh had gone upstairs to the meeting room to set up his equipment. At first he could sense a lot of activity up there. The rest of us joined him and Kevin put his computer with the SLS Camera on a desk in the front of the room. He has two: the one that is connected to his laptop; the other a handheld device resembling an iPad. While we waited for something to happen, Josh talked to the ghosts, coaxing them to give us a sign that they were with us—a knock would suffice. Opening a door would be even better. At one point he saw a shadow pass by the open door, dimming the light momentarily.

# The Haunting of the Anoka Masonic Lodge

**The room in the top picture was once Dr. Aldrich's study in Colonial Hall. The room in the bottom picture, now the Job's Daughter's room in the Masonic Lodge was originally used as the preparation room. The two rooms were once connected by a common doorway which is now closed off.** *(Photos courtesy of Tom Malone)*

It didn't happen again and we went to check out the Job's Daughter's room where it seemed to have come from. There used to be a door connecting the room to Colonial Hall on the other side, but a mirror is now where the door once was. Inside the room we could pick up the faintest scent of pipe tobacco, somewhat sweet, the kind Dr. Aldrich used to smoke.

Josh returned to the meeting room and sat down. Kevin went to check out any images that might have appeared on his computer screen. Nothing. Josh continued talking to his unseen brothers. Laurie and Tom said their goodbyes and left. Josh walked over to the door and immediately noticed a drop in temperature, indicating the proximity of an entity. Then he noticed a small orb of light moving swiftly across the floor. Later, as he was sitting down, another orb rolled down the room in front of him. Then, all was quiet.

Josh and I decided to return to the kitchen area downstairs while Kevin remained upstairs hoping to capture an image of something on his SLS. The Lodge was literally a dead zone. Nothing more happened, either upstairs or downstairs. We chatted for a while and by 11:30pm decided to call it a night.

In analyzing the events of the evening, Josh thought that the earlier DeMolay meeting might have energized the ghosts that we had first encountered. Kevin had a theory about their reluctance to show themselves. The resident spirits are the ghosts of deceased Freemasons. Since Freemasons are all brothers in spirit, they feel comfortable being with their lodge brothers in death as well as in life. Kevin is not a Freemason nor do I have any Masonic connections. Possibly, they viewed us as intruders and were not interested in making our acquaintance. I must say, however, I felt a bit disappointed for as a writer of the Anoka history columns in the *Anoka County Union Herald*, I have researched and written about many of them and would have liked this opportunity to get to know them better.

And so the evening ended. Josh and Kevin packed up their gear. Josh locked the door and the three of us formed a circle holding hands while Kevin said a prayer of protection, basically telling any wayward spirits to stay put. The last thing a paranormal investigator wants to do is take his work home with him (or her.)

However, the work had just begun. Over the next few days Josh and Kevin would be analyzing the tapes and recordings that were left running during the session. Maybe, just maybe….

**Part Two**

A week after the investigation I received the following e-mail from Kevin:

*June & Josh,*
*I have a couple of voices that I have picked up. The first is an exhale or scream just before Josh gets the chills.*

I listened to the first segment that Kevin sent me that took place in the lodge. It went like this:
Voice: *Ahhhhhhhhh*

Josh: *I heard that.*
Voice: *Ohhhhhh.*
Josh: (To Kevin and me) *You feel a cold?*
(To spirit voice) *Was that you? Come closer.*
(To Kevin and me) *Do you feel it colder?—a cooler temperature?*

E-mail from Kevin with the other file...*I hear a voice just before we leave the lodge to go downstairs.*
The second segment:
*Undistinguishable whisper*
Kevin: *Should we go downstairs?*
Josh: *We can go wherever we like.*
E-mail: *Take a listen and feel free to share your thoughts....*

The next week Kevin sent two more files. These were video files from the computer he had set up to run continuously and record any anomalies on the SLS camera.

Kevin's e-mail:

*Good evening. June, I came across a short mapping on the SLS camera. This was captured while I was sitting in the balcony. Josh mentioned seeing a shadow of someone sitting in the second row, second chair. This mapping was captured just feet away from there.*

*I will add that the mapping is along an edge in the wall, which could be a false positive. I'll let you both make up your own minds.*

*There is one more clip which I will send in a separate email. The file is rather large.*

*-Kevin*

The first clip Kevin sent was a quick glimpse of an anomaly outlined against a plane of green. The points of contact were gray squares connected by lines forming a stick figure. It was definitely moving. The second clip was lengthier. It showed fuzzy red and green images of the seats in the balcony where it was taped. The gray balcony railing is in the background where the anomaly appears to be standing and moving about a bit, but staying in one place. In this clip the outline of the ghost is captured by the camera in bright yellow squares against a plane of blue. Light blue connecting lines form the figure which at first appears to be standing as the squares and lines designating the feet and knees are parallel to one another. Then the feet cross into an X, suggesting that the entity is seated.

In the second clip the anomaly (or ghost) was sticking around longer than in the first clip, probably to listen to the ghost story Josh was telling of his encounter with the ghost of Harry Hayward, first person to be hung in the new Minneapolis Courthouse in 1895. Josh is a policeman whose job is night watch at the Minneapolis City Jail, located on the top floor of the courthouse, a place where ghosts abound.

**Kevin Swanson, Paranormal Investigator**
(Photo courtesy of Tom Malone)

## A PI and His Theory

I, Kevin Swanson, have been a paranormal investigator since 2010. As a child, I would listen to my grandmother talk about her communication with my deceased grandfather. As a child, I then began to have my own experiences that made me curious of the unexplained. Over the years, I have investigated dozens of homes, business and public venues. As a skeptic believer, I focus on using technology to confirm or debunk ghostly activity. Some of my favorite gear includes an audio voice recorder, infrared cameras, the K-2 and Mel meters, a Flir thermal camera, and the SLS camera. My goal is to determine what frequencies these events occur at so we can predict paranormal activity.

I grew up in Burnsville and now live in St. Louis Park, Minnesota with my wife and two children. Except for a short stint in California, I have lived in Minnesota my entire life. Besides Ghost Hunting, I am a Facility Manager for an Orthopaedic Clinic in Bloomington, Minnesota as well as a board member of the Burnsville Historical Society. When I am not working or investigating, I like to camp and garden.

I have been investigating the paranormal for approximately five years. During that time, I've had many strange experiences and heard many theories as to what these might be. Millions of others from around the globe also report having their own unexplained experiences. Many of these experiences can be explained with a little investigation, yet not all of them. So, what are we dealing with?

While investigating locations such as private homes, businesses, cemeteries, and a morgue, I find these experiences can be broken down into a group of categories. These are:

- Explainable phenomenon (floor boards creaking, etc... non-paranormal)
- Residual energy (the same event happening on a regular schedule)
- The spirit of someone who has died yet has not crossed over.
- The spirit of someone who has crossed over and returned (for whatever reason)
- An elemental, or entity (something that never took human form)
- A demonic, or evil, presence

In the first category, with a little investigation, we can find explainable answers to much of what we first believe to be paranormal. Someone whispers while conducting an EVP session. Floor boards may creak at night due to the house cooling. Or, a poorly grounded building causes unusually high EMF readings. If gone undetected, some people will believe they had a paranormal encounter even though high emf is known to cause headaches, nausea, and a sense of paranoia.

In the second category, residual energy is often referred to as a time loop—as if a specific event appears to play itself over and over again. This can occur daily, or nightly, such as when grandma would go down the stairs at two am every night to check if the door was locked. These occurrences can also be more infrequent such as the annual anniversary of a tragic accident or death. These recurring events seem to be stamped into our reality at a specific time and location with no changes to the pattern whatsoever.

The remaining categories are what I would classify as conscious energy. I came to this conclusion based upon the fact that we seem to share the same space as our invisible brothers and sisters. Yet, we are merely out of phase or resonating at a different frequency as they do. This can include ghosts, spirits, fairies, gnomes, and demons. Experiences that fall into this category have the ability to interact, talk, hide, and even enter our bodies, all the while, sharing the same space as us. Apparitions, electronic voice phenomena and orbs all fall into this conscious energy category.

What is this conscious energy? I like to think this energy is similar to us here in the physical world. While the Earth resonates at 7.8 hz, I believe those in the spirit world resonate at a higher frequency. This is why we cannot see them. The question is: What frequency are they at? If we can discover the answer and tune our equipment to it, we will be able to get repeated results every time we investigate.

As I continue to investigate, I search for this mysterious frequency or frequencies. Once I am locked into it, it will be easier to document interactions with the other side. This will lead me to prove my theory of conscious energy. ....*Kevin Swanson*

## Further Reading

Not surprisingly, I have a number of books on my bookshelf that deal with the paranormal. Thanks to television in part, it has become a popular genre'. Many of the books, even whole series, are anecdotal stories about haunted places such as, *Haunted Lakes, Haunted Minnesota,* and *A Guidebook to Haunted Places in the Twin Cities.*

And then there are the books written by people who actually experience first-hand the paranormal aspects of our earthly realm, people known as Ghost Whisperers. Probably the best known of them is Mary Ann Winkowski upon whose talents and experiences the popular television series, *The Ghost Whisperer*, in which Jennifer Love Hewitt plays the leading role, is based. Mary Ann tells her own story in her book, *When Ghosts Speak: Understanding the World of Earthbound Spirits.* She says, "Whether we're aware of them or not, ghosts are always among us—and they have been a part of my life since my early childhood."

James Van Praagh, another ghost whisperer, was the co-executive producer of the *Ghost Whisperer* series. Unlike Mary Ann Winkowski who sees only earthbound spirits, Van Praagh sees free spirits and describes his experiences along with explanations in his book, *Ghosts Among Us: Uncovering the Truth About the Other Side.*

Closer to home is Michael Bodine, a professional psychic whose celebrity clients included Patrick Swayze of the movie *Ghost* fame. Michael and his equally psychic sister, Echo Bodine, live in Minneapolis. His memoir, *Growing up Psychic: From Skeptic to Believer*, is well worth the read.

.

# Works Consulted

## Ghost Theory 101

*The Other Side* by Marley Gibson, Patrick Burns, and Dave Schrader

*Ghosts Among Us*: James Van Praagh

*The Spirit Book*: Raymond Buckland

## The Doctors Aldrich and Colonial Hall

*Third Avenue Elegance: Colonial Hall & the Doctors Aldrich: A History produced by the Anoka County Historical Society.*

"Dr. Flora Aldrich – a woman ahead of her time" Anoka County History by Maria King, Contributing Columnist. ABC Newspapers, July 25, 2014.

"Doctors take honeymoon trip of a lifetime" Anoka County History, June Anderson Contributing Columnist, ABC Newspapers, Feb. 20, 2015

## Who Are the Masons?

"Masonry": World Book Encyclopedia, Volume M

"A Brief History of the Masonic Order": Pietre Stones

American Masonic History, "What Are America's True Roots?" (Material excerpted from a 6/90 *Media Spotlight* Special Report –"A Masonic History of America," by Al Dager

June Gossler Anderson

"Masons and the Making of America" U.S. News

Albert M. Goodrich: *History of Anoka County*

John Freeburg, "A Brief History of Anoka Lodge No 30 A.F. & A.M. (Ancient Free and Accepted Masons)"

Appendix

# Paranormal Investigation of the Banfill-Locke House

As a docent for the Anoka County Historical Society, I have been taking people on Ghost Tours through the darkened streets of Anoka since 2007. Over the years I have often been asked if I have ever seen a ghost. Up until January 10, 2015 my answer had always been "no." That night I was part of a paranormal investigation of a well-known haunted site in Anoka County, Banfill-Locke Center for the Arts. One of the oldest dwellings in the county, it was built as a summer home in 1847 by John Banfill at the confluence of Rice Creek and the Mississippi River in Fridley. Banfill was a retired colonel in the army and Minnesota's first State Auditor. The Greek Revival Style house served as his home and office.

The road running in front of the Banfill House was part of the Red River Oxcart Trail, along which furs were hauled by oxcart from Canada to Fort Snelling and Mendota for shipment to Europe via the Mississippi, and trade goods were hauled back north. By 1852 the Army engineers had improved the trail, designating it as the Territorial Road, thus making the location of Banfill's house the perfect stopping-off point. John Banfill added on to the house and opened it as the Banfill Wayside Inn, catering to travelers and workers on the military and fur trade route.

In 1870 the house was sold to Laura Locke and William Brown who operated it as a dairy farm. In 1912 Cassius Locke bought the property and turned a portion of it over to the Girl Scouts for a Brownie Camp. In 1946, I was a Brownie attending Camp Lockslea in Fridley, Minnesota (which I was sure was somewhere along the Canadian border). One day we campers trudged down East River Road, then an unpaved dirt road that took us to the Locke house. We were going to visit old Mr. and Mrs. Locke who had given the Girl Scouts the land for our camp. The ancient couple was hospitable and charming. Mrs. Locke played the old pump organ for us and Mr. Locke told us ghost stories. I especially remember him telling us about the ghost in the closet. He died in the house the following year.

In 1988 the historic house became the home of the North Suburban Center for the Arts which hosts several art shows during the year. A very popular exhibit was last summer's "Art of Darkness" featuring paranormal works of art. I met Dave Schrader, host of Darkness Radio, at the opening reception and later signed up for a series of six classes he would be teaching on paranormal investigation through community ed. Our class culminated with a January paranormal investigation of the Banfill-Locke House. I would soon find out if there was any truth to old Mr. Locke's stories told to me so very long ago.

I envisioned a paranormal investigation as sitting quietly for hours in a dark room waiting for something to go "bump" in the night. This was entirely different. This was a high-tech investigation. Under Dave's guidance seventeen of us met at 9:00 pm in the Banfill-Locke House to check it out for "anomalies." We used the most up-to-date ghost hunting equipment which included meters that measure electro-magnetic energy, light sensors that make a fuss if something seen or unseen interrupts the beam of light, recorders that pick up ghostly whispers, and a video camera, called a Structured Light Sensor (SLS), that captures and records unseen entities. It works much the same way as the interactive game camera on your TV that allows you to play tennis and other games with it. Like sonar that bounces sound waves, the SLS camera bounces light rays off a three-dimensional figure. With a minimum of eighteen points of reference, it connects the dots to form a stick figure.

Armed and ready we spread out to explore the large dark rooms of the Banfill-Locke House. I stuck with Dave. He had a portable SLS camera. It's about the size of an iPad with a handle for grasping on the underside, the camera on its leading edge, and a viewing screen on top. We went upstairs to stand in the doorway of the director's office. As we watched the screen on the SLS, the area in front of the water cooler turned green and "anomaly sighted" flashed on the screen. Dots of light connecting up to form a stick figure appeared before the water cooler; then moved quickly off the screen. Then it came back for an encore. Dave pressed the record button.

We headed downstairs to the basement, a small space under the gift shop that contains mostly furnace. The SLS picked up glimpses of green stick figures darting around. Dave turned the camera to an alcove with a five gallon bucket in the corner, joking that if he saw an anomaly there he'd-----. Just then, a green stick figure showed up crouching over the bucket.

Kevin Swanson, another paranormal investigator, also had an SLS camera, and many of the seventeen "amateurs" were using some of the other equipment. All were getting results. One woman and her husband had borrowed Kevin's SLS and were looking for ghosts in the downstairs closets. I watched over her shoulder as the camera picked up her husband. He appeared as a stick man on the screen. Off screen, his body had form. As he opened the closet door a formless stick figure came popping out and started playing with his hair. Although the husband was unaware of the interaction, the "little green man" appeared to be having a jolly good time. (Maybe Mr. Locke hadn't been kidding after all.)

Then it was my turn. I wandered around aiming the SLS at likely looking places. Sometimes a stick figure would appear against a plane of red, or blue or green. On several occasions a regular sized stick figure was joined by a much smaller one, perhaps a child. I meandered back upstairs where reports were that they were getting lots of activity. I was recording anomalies in various locations. Dave was in the painting room. He asked us to be quiet so he could record an EVP on an Ovilus, which is a state-of-the-art ghost voice recorder. While he played the tape back I continued to look for anomalies with the SLS camera. There were a few flitting around the room. I picked up one standing menacingly over Dave as a hoarse voice coming from the Ovilus whispered, "Get Out!" With all due respect we did.

www.ingramcontent.com/pod-product-compliance
Lightning Source LLC
Chambersburg PA
CBHW071158090426
42736CB00012B/2366